THE INNER CONTROL IS THE TRUE CONTROL WORKBOOK

Making Lasting Lifestyle and Behavioral Changes

Inspirational Scripts

Second Edition

A. Sehatti, RN, MSN
Family Nurse Practitioner

NCWC/Amend-Health Press

THE INNER CONTROL IS THE TRUE CONTROL WORKBOOK: *Making Lasting Lifestyle and Behavioral Changes* **- Inspirational Scripts. Second Edition.** Copyright © 2022 by A. Sehatti, RN, MSN, Family Nurse Practitioner.

All rights reserved.

No part of this book may be reproduced in whole or in part, translated, stored in a retrieval system, or transmitted, in any form or by any means such as recording, electronic, mechanical, microfilming, or otherwise, without the prior written permission of the author (A. Sehatti, RN, MSN, FNP) or NCWC/ Amend-Health Press.

ISBN 978-0-578-37813-8 (paperback)

| Lifestyle and behavior change | Self-confidence | Eating disorders | Alcoholism |
| Addiction | Weight loss | Total wellness | Forgiveness |

Printed and bounded in the United States of America

First edition copyrighted: May 2018
Revised editions copyrighted: March 2021, December 2021

Second edition copyrighted: February 2022
Revised edition copyrighted: August 2023

Published by:
NCWC/Amend-Health Press
AKA Nutritional Counseling and Weight Control Clinic
51 E. Campbell Avenue, Suite 129 - 154
Campbell, CA 95008
United States
www.NCWC-AmendHealthPress.com

About the Author

A. Sehatti is a registered nurse and family nurse practitioner. She received her bachelor's degree in nursing from University of Pennsylvania and her master's degree in nursing from University of California, Los Angeles. Aside from her clinical work at such places as Caltech Health Center, UCLA, and Stanford Medical Center, she has over forty years of experience in educating adults and children on weight management, nutrition, and total wellness. A. Sehatti is highly dedicated to making a difference in people's lives. She currently works as a nutritional consultant and health educator at a private practice that she established in 2005 in Northern California. It has been the reward of witnessing people reach their health and wellness goals that has inspired the author to write books and share the tools that have helped her clients with her readers.

CONTENTS

About This Workbook   1

PART I: A DETERMINED, PROACTIVE, AND GOAL-ORIENTED MINDSET

Motivational Self-Talks   7
Summary   13

PART II: A FLEXIBLE, ADAPTABLE, AND TOLERANT MINDSET

Validating and Affirming Self-Talks   19
Summary   25

PART III: AN EMPOWERING AND CONSTRUCTIVE MINDSET

Empowering Self-Talks   31
Summary   39

PART IV: A SUPPORTIVE, REALISTIC, AND LOGICAL MINDSET

Nurturing Self-Talks   47
Summary   53

PART V: A MINDFUL, CONSCIENTIOUS, AND EMPATHETIC MINDSET

Perceptive Self-Talks   59
Emotional Healing   69
Summary   88

About This Workbook

> "The Inner Control Is the True Control Workbook" is a companion book to "Building a Strong Sense of Self: Embarking on the Journey of Change." Although it is recommended that one reads both books simultaneously in order to reap the maximum benefit, you may choose to read either one independently of the other—both books will help you gain awareness and make lasting behavioral and lifestyle changes.

Through offering inspirational self-talks scripts, this short and easy-to read workbook promotes the following five positive mindsets that are explored in *Building a Strong Sense of Self: Embarking on the Journey of Change*: determined, proactive, and goal-oriented; flexible and adaptable; empowering and constructive; supportive, realistic, and logical; and, mindful, conscientious, and empathetic.

Part I through Part V, which directly correspond to the five parts in *Building a Strong Sense of Self*, reinforce these mindsets by presenting the following related self-talk scripts, respectively: motivational; validating and affirming; empowering; nurturing; and, perceptive.

These inner dialogues will help you on your journey of change: they will empower you to become mindful, stay in control; stick to your self-care routine; and, achieve your health goals. Additionally, these scripts, which are crafted as such to raise your concentration and attention, will help you become present and gain a sense of inner peace and tranquility.

To trigger neuroplasticity and reach a lasting transformation, it is strongly recommended that one develop a daily routine by reading one or two scripts each day.

> For more in-depth reading on the topics covered in this workbook, please refer to its companion book, "Building a Strong Sense of Self: Embarking on the Journey of Change."

> A WORD OF CAUTION: Please be informed that "The Inner Control Is the True Control Workbook" delivers its message in a forthright manner. This approach is used intentionally in order to achieve the desired goal of breaking the wall of resistance (i.e., denial) that protects our inner wounds but makes us remain emotionally stuck. Therefore, some readers may experience a short-term inner turmoil as they work through some of the sections in this book.
>
> "It is only by going down into the abyss that we recover the treasures of life. Where you stumble, there lies your treasure." —Joseph Campbell

PART I

A DETERMINED, PROACTIVE, AND GOAL-ORIENTED MINDSET

"To make 'lasting' behavioral and lifestyle changes, we first become aware of our unhelpful thinking patterns that drive our unhealthy habits; then, we develop and cultivate a more constructive set of inner thoughts and self-talks that empowers us to gain control and make better choices.

In other words, to be able to maintain our behavioral changes and achieve our health goals, we may need to make a fundamental change in 'the way we think.'

A constructive and positive outlook that is executed by the prefrontal cortex part of our brain keeps our instinctive impulses in check and helps us stay in control and sustain our healthy lifestyle changes.

Working through the journey of change can be an uphill battle: Even when we work diligently through the process, we may still encounter challenges and revert back to our old habits.

However, when we are 'determined' to achieve our goals, make great 'efforts' to overcome challenges (i.e., temptations), and 'persevere' in the face of setbacks, then we become empowered to learn from our mistakes, commit to new ways of thinking and behaving, and move onward."

A. Sehatti, *Building a Strong Sense of Self: Embarking on the Journey of Change (1) The Inner Control Is the True Control* (Campbell, CA: NCWC/Amend-Health Press, Second edition 2022), Part I, Page 17

Motivational Self-Talks

> *Please pause a moment. Take a slow and deep breath. While reading the following script, let each sentence deep into your conscious awareness. Then, allow the Nurturing Adult within you to guide you.*

In order to change my unhealthy behaviors and habits and reach total wellness, I will practice mindfulness:

While I stay in the moment,
I connect with my inner *self* and observe myself
in a non-judgmental manner:

I become aware of my negative feelings.

Now,

As I continue to stay connected with my inner *self*
in a supportive and nurturing way,
I focus on my thoughts:

I become aware of the inner thoughts and
self-talks that have generated
my unpleasant emotions.

Now,

I replace these unhelpful thoughts and self-dialogues
with a set of constructive (e.g., empowering, nurturing,
and realistic) self-talks that would generate positive
feelings and empower me to regain control
and make healthy choices.

Now,

I commit myself to working through these steps
and practicing mindfulness on a regular basis
in order to maintain
my healthy behavioral and lifestyle changes.

As I go through the process of change and cultivate a mindset that drives healthy behaviors and results in rewarding outcomes, I will keep in mind that:

Reverting back to my old patterns of thinking
that drive my old habits is a natural part
of the journey of transformation.

However, I will remind myself that I *can* overcome regressions and relapses:

I *can* get my life back on the right path
again when I go back and retake
the steps of mindfulness.

> "Mindfulness is neither difficult nor complex; remembering to be mindful is the great challenge." —Christina Feldman

Please stay in the present moment!

> *Please pause a moment. Take a slow and deep breath. While reading the following script, let each sentence deep into your conscious awareness. Then, allow the Nurturing Adult within you to guide you.*

I understand that, on my journey of change, there may be times that I would be unable to *easily* regain my control and get my life back on the right path again when I regress to my old habits (relapse).

In such trying times, I may become frustrated, feel *stuck*, give up on my goal, and gradually return to living on autopilot and in a mechanical manner.

If that happens, I will ask myself:
"Why am I stuck?"

This self-inquiry may provoke such thoughts as the following and help me find the answer(s):

○ Is it possible that, in discovering my flaws (an essential step in the process of *true* change), I'm experiencing inner turmoil (i.e., feelings of shame and/or guilt)? If so, then could it be that I have given up on my journey in order to block out the unpleasant thoughts that generate these painful emotions?

○ In other words, is it possible that, at the subconscious level, I am resisting to deal with *the truth* and move onward?

○ If so, then could it be that I am engaging in avoidance coping because *I am not emotionally resilient*? If yes, then could this be the reason why I am stuck on my journey?

Or,

- Is it possible that I have reverted back to my old unhealthy ways of being and feel stuck because, while I am changing, others in my immediate environment (i.e., people in my social circle, such as my significant other, family, or friends) are not (since they are not going through the journey with me)?

Now,

I realize that to prevail on my journey of change
and accomplish my goals,
I need to set myself up for success.

Therefore, I will:

Build emotional resilience;
Become proactive; and,
Create a healthy environment that
would foster personal growth.

Now,

I believe in myself;
Believe in other people; and,
Support and empower others to meet me
on the journey of change.

> *Please stay
> in the present
> moment!*

> *Please pause a moment. Take a slow and deep breath. While reading the following script, let each sentence deep into your conscious awareness. Then, allow the Nurturing Adult within you to guide you.*

I now realize that achieving *lasting* behavioral and lifestyle changes requires:

Determination,
Exertion, and
Perseverance.

Now,

I will build emotional resilience:

I will believe in myself: I will separate my faulty ways of thinking and behaving (my flaws) from my *Self* (*The Person Within*).

Now,

I will choose proactivity over passivity:

I will become enlightened by gaining insight and enlighten others by expressing myself.

Now,

I will create a healthy environment that would foster personal growth:

I will focus on my own flaws and shape my environment as I lead by example.

I will believe in other people. Therefore, I will not fix;
Rather, I will support and empower others
in my environment to transform and
meet me on the continuum of personal growth.

I will remain strong and separate: I will take
equal posturing in my relationships
by maintaining my healthy boundaries.

Now,
I realize that,

*My journey with others is
effecting change together:*

*When I change, others in my immediate
environment will change;*

*When others change,
I will change.*

> "In order to change the nature
> of things, either within yourself or
> in others, one should change, not
> the events, but those thoughts which
> created those events." —Leo Tolstoy

> *Please stay
> in the present
> moment!*

Summary

To achieve lasting behavioral and lifestyle changes, I need to make a fundamental change in the way I think.

A constructive outlook helps me keep my instinctive impulses in check, stay in control, make better choices, and *sustain* my healthy behavioral and lifestyle changes.

Working through the process of change can become an uphill battle. Therefore, I need to be *determined,* make *great efforts,* and *persevere* when I face setbacks.

I understand that regressions (relapses) are a natural part of the process of change.

Now,

I will view relapses as an opportunity for further learning and growth.

Now,

When I regress to my old habits,
I will:

Hold myself accountable in a non-judgmental way,
Learn from my mistakes;
Commit to new ways of thinking and behaving; and,
Move onward.

> *Please stay
> in the present
> moment!*

Why is the process of change so difficult?

Among other reasons, changing our habits, behaviors, or lifestyle may be challenging because:

We can only change what we face: Facing our character flaws and holding ourselves accountable for our mistakes can be a long and painful undertaking. This is especially true for those of us who have used the defense mechanism of avoidance to deal with our setbacks.

Making the right choices is a balancing act: Finding answers and making right decisions can become confusing and frustrating. This is because the answers don't always lie in our head; Nor do they lie in our heart. They lie deep within us.

Change takes place during the process (this journey is not about the destination): Staying in the moment, taking small but steady steps, and persevering through adversity is not always easy. Remaining patient and resolute is particularly difficult for those of us who are motivated by immediate gains.

Growth thrives in a favorable environment: Setting ourselves up for success by creating an environment that is conducive to growth can be challenging. This task is even more difficult to achieve when people in our immediate environment remain unaware and sabotage our growth (because they feel threatened by our transformation).

Source: *Accountability and Empowerment: A Four-Step Strategy for Overcoming Resentment*

Although the journey of personal growth and transformation is challenging, we go through this life-changing process because we deserve to live a fulfilled life.

Personal transformation not only liberates us and enriches our lives but also spares the next generation from experiencing emotional suffering; For when we are more aware, we will pass down less flawed character-traits to our offspring.

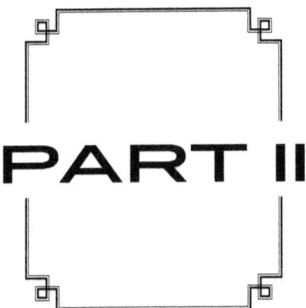

PART II

A FLEXIBLE, ADAPTABLE, AND TOLERANT MINDSET

When I focus on my own self,
I am not being self-absorbed.

When I make a healthy environment for myself,
I am not being antisocial.

When I engage in self-care,
I am not being selfish.

When I stop sacrificing my physical, mental, or
emotional needs to attend to those of others,
I am not being egocentric.

So, without being enabling,
I will be kind and understanding to the child in me;
It is only then that I can be the best I could ever be.

When I am the best that I could ever be,
then I can be patient, tolerant, and understanding.

When I am the best that I could ever be,
then I can genuinely care for other people.

When I am the best that I could ever be,
then I can give without expecting anything in return.

When I am the best that I could ever be,
then I can see that others matter, too.

So, I Matter!

A. Sehatti, *Building a Strong Sense of Self: Embarking on the Journey of Change (1) The Inner Control Is the True Control* (Campbell, CA: NCWC/Amend-Health Press, Second edition 2022), Part II, Page 38

Validating and Affirming Self-Talks

> *Please pause a moment. Take a slow and deep breath. While reading the following script, let each sentence deep into your conscious awareness. Then, allow the Nurturing Adult within you to guide you.*

I value my *self* and my existence:
I realize that I matter.

Now,

I affirm and acknowledge my *total self*:

I appreciate the *innate traits* that
I have inherited; and,

I take ownership of the *character traits*
(ways of thinking, feeling, and behaving)
that I have acquired through learning.

Now,

I acknowledge my inner *thoughts* and self-talks:
I realize that my thoughts matter.

I acknowledge the way
I observe the world around me:
I realize that these perceptions that shape my realities
(the way I interpret my experiences) matter.

Therefore,

I will no longer dismiss my own thoughts,
opinions, ideas, beliefs, or perceptions;

Instead,

I will observe my internal thoughts and dialogues
in a non-judgmental way;

I will evaluate my opinions and ideas with
a realistic and reasonable mindset;

I will examine my beliefs with
an open mind; and,

I will check my perceptions and realities
in an objective and impartial manner
and seek the truth.

Now,

I acknowledge all my *feelings*:

I realize that I feel a wide range of emotions
that is a natural part of the human experience.

I understand that all human emotions and
feelings (including jealousy and hatred)
are *real*, *valid*, and *acceptable*.

I realize that my negative feelings become dysfunctional
only when I don't deal with them in a healthy manner
(i.e., when I act upon them and become *reactive* or
when I bottle up and become *passive*).

This understanding mindset
allows me to validate *all* my feelings
in a non-critical and non-judgmental manner.

Therefore,

I will no longer dismiss or repress such
painful emotions as shame or guilt;

Nor will I bottle up or become self-critical
when I feel rage, envy, or hatred;

Instead,

I will allow myself to feel all
my emotions;

I will take ownership of the way
I feel these emotions; and,

I will heal all my negative feelings by discovering
and resolving their root cause.

Now,

I acknowledge my physical, mental,
emotional, and spiritual *needs*:

I realize that all my fundamental
human needs matter.

Therefore,

I will no longer dismiss or neglect what I need in order
to be physically, mentally, or emotionally healthy;

Instead,

I will attend to all my basic human needs
in a responsible manner.

Now,

I acknowledge all my basic
human *rights*:

I realize that the rightful expectations that
I have of other people matter (i.e., I expect others
to treat me fairly, equally, and respectfully).

Therefore,

I will no longer neglect or disregard my fair,
reasonable, and realistic expectations;

Instead,

I will *define, set, and maintain*
a set of healthy limits and expectations
and expect others to respect them.

Now,

I acknowledge my *hopes*:

I realize that my positive and realistic aspirations
that help me reach my full potential matter.

Therefore,

I will no longer overlook my hopes, healthy and
constructive desires, or dreams;

Instead,

I will make plans, reach my goals,
and fulfill my vision.

> *Please stay
> in the present
> moment!*

> *Please pause a moment. Take a slow and deep breath. While reading the following script, let each sentence deep into your conscious awareness. Then, allow the Nurturing Adult within you to guide you.*

Now that I am able to acknowledge and affirm my *self*, I am empowered to validate and affirm other people:

Now,

I appreciate and respect other people's basic human rights:

I realize that everyone has a right to exist and survive; and,

I acknowledge that the life and well-being of every individual matters.

Now,

I acknowledge people's *total self*:

I affirm the *innate traits* that they have inherited;

and,

I validate the *character traits* (ways of thinking, feeling, and behaving) that they have acquired through learning.

Therefore,

I will no longer dismiss or disregard other people's thoughts, beliefs, or perceptions;

Instead, I will listen earnestly to
the opinions, perspectives, and realities
of others even when I strongly disagree with them.

I will no longer minimize, dismiss, or disregard
anyone's feelings;
Instead, I will become more mindful of people's
experiences and feelings.

I will no longer become careless or indifferent
towards other people's needs;
Instead, I will pay more attention and
become more aware of the needs of others
(e.g., I will help, support, and empower vulnerable
individuals to meet their own basic human needs).

I will no longer ignore or dismiss people's
reasonable and fair expectations;
Instead, I will become more mindful of others'
requests, concerns, and personal boundaries.

I will no longer dismiss people's positive
and forward-looking ideas, hopes, and aspirations
that motivate them to reach their full potential;
Instead, I will support and empower
others to reach their vision.

> *Please stay
> in the present
> moment!*

Summary

Now that I am more enlightened, I validate and value the *total person* in me:

I matter.
I am good enough: I am inherently worthy.
My opinions, realities, feelings, needs,
fair expectations, and hopes matter.

Now,

I stay true to my own sound principles, beliefs, and values because I have a strong sense of my *self*.

Now,

I no longer harbor such self-talks as:

"I should think, feel, or behave in a certain way
so that everyone would acknowledge me, like me,
approve of me, or regard me as worthy."

Now,

I am able to acknowledge and affirm my *self*.

❧ ❧ ❧

Validating and valuing myself empowers me to acknowledge and affirm other people:

Everyone matters.
Every single individual is inherently worthy.
Others' feelings, opinions, realities, needs,
fair expectations, and hopes matter.

Now,

I validate other people's feelings and acknowledge their opinions, values, and beliefs even when I strongly disagree with them.

Now,

I understand that other people have a right to feel and think the way they do.

Now,

I no longer make such *demands* as:

"Others *should* think, feel, or behave in a certain way so that I could respect them or regard them as adequate or worthy."

> *Please stay in the present moment!*

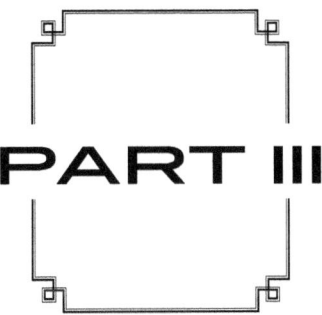

PART III

AN EMPOWERING AND CONSTRUCTIVE MINDSET

An empowering and constructive mindset that is based on 'logical principles, free will, and virtues' drives healthy actions and positive change and motivates us to engage in responsible self-care, attain total wellness, and enjoy rewarding experiences.

A. Sehatti, *Building a Strong Sense of Self: Embarking on the Journey of Change (1) The Inner Control Is the True Control* (Campbell, CA: NCWC/Amend-Health Press, Second edition 2022), Part III, Page 57

The Inherent Mindset of Natural and Healthy Children

I matter; No one else matters!
I'm important; No one is as important as me!
I'm special; No one is as special as me!
My needs matter; No one's needs are greater than mine!

I have to get what I want, the way I want it, and when I want it! I want what I want now! I'm only interested in instant gratification; I don't care what happens later.

I only want to play, have fun, and experience pleasure. I experience pleasure when I get what I want; receive attention, approval, praise, or reward; when I'm right; or, when I win ...

When I experience pleasure, I feel safe, loved, and protected. When I feel safe and secure, then I will smile at you and love you because I feel happy.

I don't like to feel displeasure. I experience displeasure when I'm neglected; can't get what I want; am held accountable, controlled, or kept from doing what I want to do... These unpleasant experiences make me feel unloved and insecure—like I'm not good enough.

When I feel unloved and insecure, I will not like you. I will cry and throw a tantrum to punish and control you (so that I get what I want). When I get what I want, then I will be happy again; Then, I will like you.

I'm defenseless and helpless:
I need to be defended, protected, and taken care of.

I'm fragile and need to avoid displeasure.
Therefore, I will do anything to avoid punishment.

I'm special: I need to experience pleasure.
Therefore, I will please you and do all of those things that would bring rewards.

A. Sehatti, *Building a Strong Sense of Self: Embarking on the Journey of Change (1) The Inner Control Is the True Control* (Campbell, CA: NCWC/Amend-Health Press, Second edition 2022), Part III, Page 44

Empowering Self-Talks

> *Please pause a moment. Take a slow and deep breath. While reading the following script, let each sentence deep into your conscious awareness. Then, allow the Nurturing Adult within you to guide you.*

The insight that I have gained into myself gives me the clarity to see *Me*.

Now,

When I look in the mirror, I no longer see a distorted image of my *self* that was projected onto me by others in the past.

Now, I see that:

I am neither inferior nor superior;

I am equal to others; and,

I *am* adequate.

Now,

I live my life being *Me*:

Unafraid of being judged, rejected, or abandoned by others.

Unafraid of other people's angry or retaliatory responses.

Now,

I don't need other people to:
Like me,
Notice me,
Accept me,
Acknowledge me,
Approve of me, or
Admire or praise me to know that
I am worthy or that I matter.

Now,

I am aware that, as a mature adult, it is my responsibility to affirm and validate myself:
*I am good enough; I do matter; and,
I am worthy of being loved.*

Now,

I love my 'self' unconditionally.

No one is special. I don't need others' affirmation that I am special to think that I'm adequate. I *am* good enough!

I don't have to fit in to be good enough; I *am* good enough!

My mistakes don't define Me. I don't have to be perfect to be good enough. I *am* good enough!

Now, I will stop being hard on myself.

---

*Please stay
in the present
moment!*

> *Please pause a moment. Take a slow and deep breath. While reading the following script, let each sentence deep into your conscious awareness. Then, allow the Nurturing Adult within you to guide you.*

I am now empowered to take
control of my life:

Now,

I stay secure and strong and
resolve my conflicts by expressing myself
in an assertive manner;

I communicate my thoughts, realities, and feelings:

*Directly, clearly, sincerely, and openly,
in a non-reactive and non-provocative manner,
with a gentle tone of voice, while maintaining a
relaxed posture and making eye contact that projects
kindness, confidence, and strength.*

Now,

I protect myself in a healthy and
effective manner:

I *establish* a set of healthy personal boundaries
in my relationships;

I *define* these limits clearly, firmly, and
respectfully; and,

I *maintain* my personal boundaries
consistently.

Now,

I make an honest appraisal of my faulty ways of thinking, feeling, and behaving (my character flaws) and see my own part in my emotional suffering without being critical or judgmental towards myself:

I separate my character flaws from my *Self (The Person Within)*;

Therefore, I no longer label my *'self'* as bad, inadequate, inferior . . .

Now,

I lead a proactive life:

I commit to learning new and improved ways of thinking, feeling, and behaving that fit the true *Me*.

I focus on learning healthy ways to deal with setbacks and negative emotions.

I engage in responsible self-care.

I create a positive and healthy environment that fosters personal growth.

Now,

I see my inner strength.

Please stay in the present moment!

> *Please pause a moment. Take a slow and deep breath. While reading the following script, let each sentence deep into your conscious awareness. Then, allow the Nurturing Adult within you to guide you.*

Now, I allow the Nurturing Adult within me to govern my internal thoughts, self-talks, feelings, and behaviors towards other people.

Now,

I will treat others the way I would like to be treated:

I will love my loved ones *unconditionally*.

I will separate people's faulty ways of thinking, feeling, and behaving (their character flaws) from their *Self* (*The Person Within*); Therefore, I will not label others as good or bad, normal or abnormal, or superior or inferior.

I will face the truth (i.e., see my character flaws) and own my negative emotions; Therefore, I will not blame or take my frustration on other people.

I will respect others' basic human rights.

I will respect the *healthy* limits that are set for me in my interpersonal relationships.

I will follow the rules of the community in which I choose to be part of.

I will lead by example;
Therefore, I will inspire people and bring about positive change in my environment.

Now,

I see my inner goodness.

> *Please stay in the present moment!*

> *Please pause a moment. Take a slow and deep breath. While reading the following script, let each sentence deep into your conscious awareness. Then, allow the Nurturing Adult within you to guide you.*

While I commit to implementing positive changes in my life and my ways of being (i.e., my ways of thinking, feeling, and behaving), I will keep in mind that, in the face of setbacks and challenges, I may not be able to fully sustain this transformation.

Now,
I accept that returning to my old ways during stressful times are a natural part of the process of change.

Now,
I realize that I'm always a work-in-progress.

This realistic outlook empowers me to push through and never give up.

Now,
I know that by taking a few small steps at a time I can regain my personal power.

Now,
I am empowered to make realistic goals and work towards progression, not perfection.

> *Please stay in the present moment!*

> *Please pause a moment. Take a slow and deep breath. While reading the following script, let each sentence deep into your conscious awareness. Then, allow the Nurturing Adult within you to guide you.*

Now,
I believe in myself.
Therefore, I will lead a proactive life.

Now,
I face the truth.
Therefore, I will see choices.

Now,
I don't wish; *I hope.*
Therefore, I will achieve my goals.

Hope inspires *resolution*, drives *exertion*, builds *resilience*, and brings *success*.

When I earnestly hope to achieve a goal then I will become determined to succeed.

This firm resolution will drive constructive behaviors: I will make *concrete plans* and exert myself to stay committed to them.

When I stick to my plans and reap the rewards of it, I will start believing in myself and become inspired to stay strong and persevere in the face of setbacks.

This is how my hopes and aspirations empower me to fulfill my vision and reach my full potential.

> *Please stay in the present moment!*

Summary

Now that I am more empowered and allow the *Adult in Me* to govern my mindset, my inner thoughts and self-talks will be like these:

I matter;
My opinions, realities, feelings,
needs, fair expectations,
and hopes matter.

I am not superior or inferior to anyone;
I am unique and worthy
of being loved.

I'm secure;
I am good enough.

I'm strong;
I am not helpless, powerless, or stuck.

I'm separate;
I have healthy personal boundaries.

I am free;
I have choices.

I'm resilient;
I can face the truth, overcome
setbacks and challenges,
and regain my inner control.

I'm self-disciplined;
I can regulate my emotions and control
my impulses and temptations.

I'm empathic;
I can understand and relate to the feelings
and experiences of other people.

I'm forgiving;
I can let go of my anger and
reach inner calmness.

I'm giving;
I have a purpose greater than myself.

I'm proactive;
I can reach my full potential.

I'm ethical and conscientious;
I am responsible towards myself,
other people, animals, and
my environment.

I believe in myself;
I am real and live an authentic life.

I'm realistic;
I'm always a work-in-progress.

As a mature adult:

It is my responsibility to meet my
basic human needs;
I am responsible for my own
shelter and food;

I'm responsible for my own physical
and emotional health and
well-being;

SUMMARY

It is my responsibility to
acknowledge and affirm myself;

It is my responsibility to resolve my own
negative feelings and problems;

It is my responsibility to protect and defend my
basic human rights; I'm responsible for defining and
maintaining my personal boundaries;

I'm responsible for the choices and
decisions that I make; and,

I'm responsible for my own happiness.

> *Please stay
> in the present
> moment!*

> The foundation for assertive communications:
>
> 1) Stay true to yourself and others.
>
> 2) Have faith in people and believe in their inherent (human) ability to deal with harsh truths.
>
> 3) Being nice # Being kind.
>
> 4) An authentic, straightforward, and direct style of communication that comes from a place of humility is *kind, respectful, and helpful*.

> Taking control of our inner thoughts and self-talks will empower us to manage our emotions, control our behaviors, sustain our healthy lifestyle changes, reach a state of equanimity, and achieve our wellness goals.
>
> "Sow a thought, and you reap an act;
> Sow an act, and you reap a habit;
> Sow a habit, and you reap a character;
> Sow a character, and you reap a destiny."
>
> —Samuel Smiles

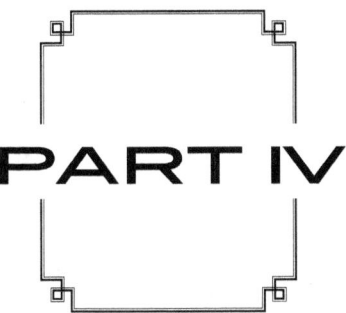

PART IV

**A SUPPORTIVE, REALISTIC,
AND LOGICAL MINDSET**

"While I cherish my strengths and take pride in my accomplishments, I realize that my advantages, greatness, gifts, talents, or skills do not define me or make me superior.

While I support myself in turning my weaknesses into my strengths, I realize that my imperfections, flaws, or limitations do not define me or make me inferior."

A. Sehatti, *Building a Strong Sense of Self: Embarking on the Journey of Change (1) The Inner Control Is the True Control* (Campbell, CA: NCWC/Amend-Health Press, Second edition 2022), Part II, Page 29

Nurturing Self-Talks

> *Please pause a moment. Take a slow and deep breath. While reading the following script, let each sentence deep into your conscious awareness. Then, allow the Nurturing Adult within you to guide you.*

I now understand that there is no path to total wellness when I define or evaluate my value or worth as a person based on external factors, such as my physical attributes, accomplishments, or what others think of me. Now, I realize:

I don't have to be thin or physically fit
in order to be good enough.

I don't have to be accomplished
in order to be adequate.

I don't have to be right, win arguments, or
be all knowing in order to be worthy.

I don't have to please other people in order
to know that I'm good and adequate.

I don't have to fix or take care of others in
order to know that I matter.

I don't have to receive attention or be acknowledged
by others to know that I am worthy.

I don't have to fit in, be popular, or be affirmed
(i.e., receive approval or praise) by those in my
social circle to know that I'm good enough.

Now,

I no longer define or evaluate my value or worth as a person based on flawed values that I learned in the early years of my childhood.

Now,

I no longer see an image of my *self* that was projected onto me by other people in my past.

Now,

When I look in the mirror,
I see a true image of *Me*.

I see that I *always* mattered; I was *always* good enough;
If others didn't see it,
it was because they had learned to evaluate
the value or worth of others
(including their own) based on flawed principles;
Therefore, they didn't know any better.

Now that I see a true image of *Me*, I realize that:

I am adequate, unique, and worthy of being treated with respect, dignity, and equality whether I am:

Thin or overweight;
Fair-skinned or dark-skinned;
Tall or short;
Young or old;
Wealthy or poor;
Popular or unpopular; or,
Educated or uneducated.

Now that I realize I am inherently worthy and good enough, I feel compassion for myself and *love my 'self' unconditionally.*

This self-love that comes from *the Nurturing Adult Within* stops me from neglecting or depreciating myself.

Now, I will allow well-thought-out principles, sound values, and virtues of humanity and love to serve as the foundation on which I build a sense of identity and define my strengths and weaknesses.

This positive mindset will generate nurturing inner thoughts and self-talks and drive constructive behaviors.

Now,
I am empowered to:

Better myself;
Create a safe environment for myself;
Maintain rewarding interpersonal relationships;
Engage in a healthy lifestyle; and,
Achieve total wellness.

> *Please stay in the present moment!*

POSITIVE SELF-IMAGE:
We see the true image of our *self*:
*"I am good enough;
I do matter."*
▼

GENUINE SELF-LOVE:
We like ourselves.
▼

SELF-COMPASSION:
We care about our *self*
and well-being.
▼

SELF-CARE:
We take care of our
physical, mental, and
emotional health.

> *Please pause a moment. Take a slow and deep breath. While reading the following script, let each sentence deep into your conscious awareness. Then, allow the Nurturing Adult within you to guide you.*

The self-compassion that comes from the Nurturing Adult within me empowers me to open my heart to other people.

Now,

I don't define or evaluate other people's value or worth as a person based on external factors, such as their physical attributes, accomplishments, wealth, race, or social status.

People are good enough whether they are thin or overweight.

They are good enough whether their skin is fair or dark.

They matter whether they are tall or short.

They are worthy whether they are young or old.

They are good enough whether they are well-educated or not-educated.

They matter whether they are wealthy or poor.

Now,

People don't have to be physically attractive to have my attention.

They don't have to be accomplished to receive my admiration.

They don't have to be winners to have my praise.

They don't have to be popular, wealthy, or powerful to have my respect.

Now,

I can see a true image of other people (*the person within*).

Now,

I can relate better to people's experiences and feelings.

This human connection and understanding mindset generates compassion in me and stops me from judging or devaluing other people.

Now,

I feel compassion for all humans.

> *Please stay in the present moment!*

Summary

Now that I am more enlightened, I realize that I don't have to possess certain physical attributes, come from a certain socioeconomic or ethnic background, be wealthy, have a college degree, or be prestigious in order to feel that I am enough or deserving of being treated with respect, justice, and fairness.

Now, I realize that I don't have to please others in order to feel worthy or adequate. I don't have to overfunction, fix, give, or take care of other people in order to think that I am good and deserving of their love.

As I extend this compassion towards other people, I no longer judge others and evaluate their value or worth based on external factors, such as their physical attributes, wealth, accomplishments, prestige, faith, or race.

I now define and evaluate myself and others based
on sound principles, values, and virtues.

I now appraise my own behaviors or those of
others based on our level of awareness.

Adopting this positive mindset helps me:
Build a stronger sense of my *self*; and,
Be more understanding and
forgiving towards other people.

Now,

*I experience a sense of serenity, equanimity,
and inner peace.*

> It may be a human phenomenon that we care about what other people think of us.
>
> To what extent, though, do we allow 'what others think of us' to define us?

> When we are *emotionally dependent* and need others to affirm us (that *we are good enough*) or acknowledge us (that *we matter or are important*), then we may have to work hard to please others and make them happy.
>
> In such a case as this, how could we ever stay true (to ourselves or others) and live a fulfilled life?
>
> *Retain your personal power:*
> *Believe in yourself.*
> *Affirm and acknowledge yourself.*

PART V

A MINDFUL, CONSCIENTIOUS, AND EMPATHETIC MINDSET

"Sometimes, to build ourselves up, we may have to first tear down the defective house that was built for us in the early years of our childhood. However, many of us live on autopilot and may not realize that the house we have been living in is, in fact, defective.

Sometimes, we may need to hear this harsh truth directly, straightforwardly, and in a forthright manner so that we gain awareness, rebuild, and better ourselves.

Naturally then, to reconstruct a house that would reflect a healthier image of our 'self' may be a painful task to accomplish.

However, we can heal our painful emotions.
We can take on the challenging task of transformation.
We can form a healthy sense of our self.

We go through this difficult process because
we deserve to live a fulfilled life."

Sehatti, A. (August 2021). *Food for Thought Newsletter,*
Nutritional Counseling & Weight Control Clinic

Perceptive Self-Talks

> *Please pause a moment. Take a slow and deep breath. While reading the following script, let each sentence deep into your conscious awareness. Then, allow the Nurturing Adult within you to guide you.*

In order to heal my emotional pain, I need to attend to my inner wounds. To do so, I first have to identify and remove my conditioned defense mechanisms.

Naturally, then, I will experience inner turmoil during the early phases of the process.

*I would experience discomfort when I rip off
the bandage of an unhealed deep wound;
In the same way,
I will experience inner unrest when I remove the
conditioned defense mechanisms that have covered
my deep inner wounds and
protected me from feeling emotional pain.*

However, I will persevere and remain determined and focused on my journey of change because I understand that the long-term reward outweighs the short-term pain.

"*What you feel, you can heal.*" —John Gray
"*What you resist will persist.*" —Carl Jung

> *Please stay in the present moment!*

> *Please pause a moment. Take a slow and deep breath. While reading the following script, let each sentence deep into your conscious awareness. Then, allow the Nurturing Adult within you to guide you.*

I realize that I was not born with my character traits: I have *learned* the ways in which I think, feel, express myself and cope with my problems. This realization helps me see that:

My flawed character traits
(my faulty patterns of thinking, feeling, and behaving)
that I learned in the early years of my childhood
do not define or limit me.

Now, I understand that as long as I live and interact with my environment, I act upon it and change it;

Accordingly, as the environment that I live in (i.e., the people around me) responds to me, I transform.

Therefore, through this never-ending process, I have the opportunity to change, grow, and reach my optimal potential.

These realizations allow me to see choices; inspire me to lead a proactive life; empower me to face my shortcomings and learn from my mistakes; and motivate me to surround myself with people who bring out the best in me.

> *Please stay in the present moment!*

> *Please pause a moment. Take a slow and deep breath. While reading the following script, let each sentence deep into your conscious awareness. Then, allow the Nurturing Adult within you to guide you.*

The knowledge that I'm constantly changing while interacting with my environment helps me realize that *I am not a fixed entity; I am always in a state of being.*

This realization stops me from labeling myself when I think, feel, or behave in a maladaptive manner.

Although I understand that reducing myself to labels is unfair, limiting, and damaging, I acknowledge that when I remain unaware and live on autopilot, I may be judged and labeled by others for my *mindless ways of being.*

Therefore, now,
I will choose to be more mindful:

Without being self-judgmental, I will observe my *self* and identify my flawed ways of thinking that drive my maladaptive behaviors (i.e., my faulty coping strategies);

I will label these defensive behaviors as they are (i.e., aggressive, passive-aggressive, or passive); and,

I will commit to new ways of being: I will change my defense mechanisms (my ways of behaving) by changing my ways of thinking—*I will change my mindset.*

> *Please stay in the present moment!*

> *Please pause a moment. Take a slow and deep breath. While reading the following script, let each sentence deep into your conscious awareness. Then, allow the Nurturing Adult within you to guide you.*

Although I know that I can change my character traits, I realize that some of my ways of thinking and behaving may have become deeply programmed in me; Therefore, some of my faulty habits may be difficult to change.

This awareness helps me become more realistic and more patient and understanding towards myself:

Since some of my character flaws may be deeply conditioned in me, it may be unrealistic to think that I would never regress to my old ways of being.

Therefore, now, I will set myself up for success: I will make realistic goals and form such constructive self-talks as:

The process of maturation and emotional growth is not about how many times I revert back to my old faulty habits (i.e., relapse); It is about how soon I will pull myself up.

Now, I will commit to facing setbacks, learning from mistakes, and moving onward.

> *Please stay in the present moment!*

> *Please pause a moment. Take a slow and deep breath. While reading the following script, let each sentence deep into your conscious awareness. Then, allow the Nurturing Adult within you to guide you.*

The realization that other people were not born with their character traits helps me realize that:

*People's flawed character traits
(their faulty patterns of thinking, feeling, and behaving)
that they learned in the early years of their
childhood do not define or limit them.*

Now,

I'm aware that others are constantly
changing while they are interacting with
their environment (i.e., *Me*);
I understand that people are always
in a *state of being*.

This awareness offers me hope
and inspires me to be an agent of change.

Now,

I will commit to being a positive force
in the lives of others:

I will lead by example.

I will enlighten, support, and empower
other people through *sharing* my insights and
observations in a non-judgmental manner.

Moreover, the realization that others are not fixed entities and that they are always in *a state of being* stops me from judging people on their faulty ways of thinking, feeling, or behaving.

Now,
*I acknowledge that limiting and reducing others
to labels is unfair and damaging.*

Now,
When I hold people accountable for violating
my healthy personal boundaries, I will take issue
with their flawed character-traits, not them.

Now,
I will identify and label other people's
faulty behaviors, not them.

Although I understand that others can transform and change their *learned character-traits*, I will keep in mind that, just like me, some of people's ways of thinking, coping, and behaving may have become deeply programmed in them, as though they were ingrained.

This awareness helps me become more patient and tolerant towards other people while I remain kind and responsible towards myself.

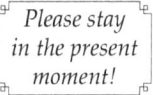
*Please stay
in the present
moment!*

> *Please pause a moment. Take a slow and deep breath. While reading the following script, let each sentence deep into your conscious awareness. Then, allow the Nurturing Adult within you to guide you.*

Now that I have gained a more understanding and empathetic mindset, I will no longer set unrealistic goals or hold myself to extremely high standards. At the same time, I will not underfunction.

Now,

I will establish a set of logical and reasonable expectations for myself that are based on excellence and not perfection;

I will commit to reaching my realistic goals by making plans and doing my best; and,

While remaining non-judgmental, I will hold myself accountable for my mistakes.

Now,

I will extend this understanding and constructive mindset towards other people:

I will not impose my unrealistic standards of perfection on other people.

I will not hold others to extremely high standards.

I will not have unrealistic expectations of my loved ones.

Now:

*I will hold others equally responsible to
the same realistic, constructive, and reasonable
expectations that I set for myself.*

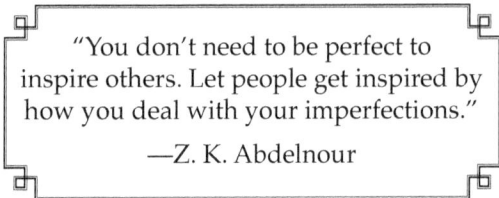

"You don't need to be perfect to
inspire others. Let people get inspired by
how you deal with your imperfections."

—Z. K. Abdelnour

*Please stay
in the present
moment!*

Holding ourselves accountable for our part in our conflicts doesn't mean that we lead a passive life:

It doesn't mean that we stop ourselves from holding others accountable; Nor does it mean that we stop ourselves from expressing our thoughts, observations, or feelings.

On the contrary, when we focus on our own mistakes (rather than those of others), we become empowered to retake our personal power and lead a proactive life.

For example, when we look inwardly and realize that we don't generally express ourselves directly or sincerely because we fear other people's judgment, rejection, abandonment, or angry reactions, we become empowered to assert ourselves and resolve problems more effectively.

Our self-discoveries that is gained through self-accountability empowers us to stay in control of our lives.

Source: Sehatti, A. (2020). *Accountability and Empowerment: A Four-Step Strategy for Overcoming Resentment (2) The Inner Control Is the True Control.* Campbell, CA: NCWC/Amend-Health Press.

What Is Empathy?

Empathy is understanding why others think, feel, or behave the way they do. This understanding comes from the compassion in our heart and is filtered through the thinking brain in our head. In other words, empathy is accepting others' humanness without pitying them or condoning their hurtful behaviors.

Moreover, empathy is a prerequisite for achieving lasting forgiveness. True forgiveness is a prerequisite for experiencing a genuine state of inner harmony and equanimity.

Understanding and accepting others' humanness and forgiving them for their wrongdoings towards us does not mean that we stick by and get hurt time and time again.

In sum, empathy is an essential ingredient for emotional healing and a key for living a life free of emotional pain.

Source: Sehatti, A. (2020). *Accountability and Empowerment: A Four-Step Strategy for Overcoming Resentment (2) The Inner Control Is the True Control.* Campbell, CA: NCWC/Amend-Health Press.

Nothing may help us feel more grounded than facing our own humanness. Nothing may help us forgive more readily than accepting other people's humanness.

Humility is a state of mind: True humility is founded on unassuming internal thoughts and self-talks. Lasting forgiveness is rooted in humility.

Emotional Healing

> *Please pause a moment. Take a slow and deep breath. While reading the following script, let each sentence deep into your conscious awareness. Then, allow the Nurturing Adult within you to guide you.*

I understand that emotional healing is a process that begins with self-awareness: *Why do I do what I do that leads to painful emotions and negative outcomes?*

I realize that when I make sense of my experiences and develop empathy towards myself, I become empowered to accept my humanness and forgive myself for my past mistakes.

This acceptance and forgiveness helps me connect to other people, relate to their experiences, and gain insight into them (understand why they do what they do).

This is when I become empowered to forgive others for their past wrongdoing and reach emotional healing.

Now, even in situations in which it feels impossible to forgive a troubled person who has victimized and wronged me, I will choose to do so. I will forgive because I deserve to experience the true inner calmness that forgiveness brings into my life.

> *Please stay in the present moment!*

> *Please pause a moment. Take a slow and deep breath. While reading the following script, let each sentence deep into your conscious awareness. Then, allow the Nurturing Adult within you to guide you.*

I realize that as a human being,
I can never be perfect.

This acknowledgment allows me to accept
my imperfections and flaws (my humanness).

Now,

I no longer judge, criticize, or blame
myself for my past mistakes.

I now understand that before undertaking
the journey of personal growth, I had
limited resources within me:

*I had remained unaware and
didn't know any better.*

This understanding state of mind
empowers me to become more
forgiving towards myself.

Now,

I forgive myself for my past wrongdoings.

> *Please pause a moment. Take a slow and deep breath. While continuing to read the following script, let each sentence deep into your conscious awareness. Then, allow the Nurturing Adult within you to guide you.*

Now that I have accepted my humanness, I no longer experience feelings of *remorse* when I make a mistake.

Now,

I don't allow the emotion of shame to turn my focus inwardly and drive my behaviors:

Now, I don't become self-absorbed and preoccupied with my own feelings of shame so much so that I become neglectful or careless towards the feelings of others.

Now,
When I make a mistake:

I don't blame myself.

I don't shift the blame: I don't project my own feelings of shame and/or guilt onto other people.

I don't distort my reality (i.e., rationalize or deny my wrongdoing) and enable myself to make the same mistake.

I don't turn to food, alcohol, or other substances in order to gain comfort and avoid facing the problem.

Now,
When I make a mistake:

I experience feelings of *regret*:
I feel sad and disappointed that
I was *being* mindless.

In doing so, I take issue with my flawed way of thinking and behaving—not with my *self*.

This conscientious and constructive state of mind helps me to forgive myself and empowers me to:

Face my wrongdoing;
Hold myself accountable for the consequences;
Express regret and offer apology in a
sincere manner (when it is needed); and,
Learn from my mistake.

Now,

I commit to learning, growing, and becoming
the best version of myself:

I establish a set of logical and reasonable
beliefs and values;
I allow these sound principles
to govern my mindset.

These new ways of thinking and internal dialogues generate healthy behaviors that would fit the true *Me*.

Now,

I realize that my imperfections or mistakes
do not define or devalue me as a person.

Now, I know that *I am good enough*.

> *Please stay
> in the present
> moment!*

> *Please pause a moment. Take a slow and deep breath. While reading the following script, let each sentence deep into your conscious awareness. Then, allow the Nurturing Adult within you to guide you.*

I understand that, as human beings, no one can ever be perfect. This awareness allows me to be more accepting, understanding, and forgiving towards other people's imperfections and flaws (their humanness).

Now,

I realize that people's flawed character-traits (their faulty patterns of thinking, feeling, and behaving) that they learned in the early years of their childhood do not define who they truly are.

Now,

I understand that before undertaking the journey of personal growth, people have limited inner resources:

We just don't know any better when we remain unaware.

This understanding state of mind empowers me to become more forgiving towards others.

Now, I forgive other people for their past wrongdoings towards me.

> *Please continue to allow your Inner Nurturing Adult to guide you while reading the following script.*

Now,
When I'm wronged:

I don't judge,
hold onto the feelings of resentment,
form a victim mentality or create a list of grievances;

I no longer allow the feelings of resentment (i.e., anger, rage, or hatred) to control and drive my behaviors.

Now,
When I'm wronged:

I don't take people's hurtful behaviors personally; Instead, I look deeper to find out and understand the truth and then, I act accordingly.

Now,
When I'm wronged,
my self-talks are like these:

Why is this person violating my
basic human rights?

Could it be that this individual has difficulty regulating their emotions or impulses because they never learned healthy ways of coping with their feelings, urges, or impulses?

Could it be that this person has a poor understanding of personal boundaries because they didn't grow up with great role models?; Or,

Could it be that this individual is troubled because they had a traumatic or difficult childhood?

Now,
When I'm wronged by others:

*I reject other people's flawed character-traits,
not them.*

> *Please pause a moment. Take a slow
> and deep breath. While continuing to read the
> following script, let each sentence deep into your
> conscious awareness. Then, allow the Nurturing
> Adult within you to guide you.*

Although I now accept others' humanness and forgive them for their wrongdoings towards me, I understand that forgiveness does *not* mean *passivity*:

Now, I realize that:

Forgiveness does not mean that
I condone abusive behaviors;
Nor doesn't it mean that I go back or
that I stick by and get hurt again and again.

Now,

While I forgive those who have wronged me,
I identify with my own experiences and feelings.
This self-awareness and self-empathy
empowers me to lead a *proactive life*.

Now,

I hold others accountable for their wrongdoings towards me by expressing myself in an assertive way:

I communicate my thoughts, realities, and feelings
directly, firmly, and respectfully,
in a non-reactive and non-provocative manner.

I defend and protect myself by establishing,
setting, and maintaining a set of clear, solid,
and healthy personal boundaries.

Now, I will retake my personal power.

"When people are not able to control you, they control how others view you." —Unknown

"Sometimes people pretend you're a bad person so that they don't feel guilty for how they treated you." —Unknown

"When another person makes you suffer, it is because they suffer deeply within themselves and their suffering is spilling over. They do not need punishment; they need help. That's the message they are sending." Source—Thich Nhat Hanh"

"Your greatest test will be how you handle people who mishandled you."—Buddha

Retake your personal power! Your emotional experiences don't have to result in emotional suffering: Stay strong but Forgive.

Please stay in the present moment!

> *Please pause a moment. Take a slow and deep breath. While reading the following script, let each sentence deep into your conscious awareness. Then, allow the Nurturing Adult within you to guide you.*

Now, the empathy that comes from the Nurturing Adult within me empowers me to open my heart to my parents (or parent figures) and extend my compassion and understanding mindset to them.

Now,

I understand that, as human beings, my parents could have never been perfect people or perfect parents.

Now,

I understand that, just like me, my parents learned many of their flawed patterns of thinking, feeling, and behaving during the early years of their childhood.

These acknowledgments allow me to become more accepting of my parents' imperfections and flaws (their humanness).

Accepting my parents' humanness is liberating: Now, I no longer have the need to fix or change my parents.

Now,

I am free to search and discover the truth.

> *Please continue to allow your Inner Nurturing Adult to guide you while reading the following script.*

Now, when I look back on my childhood and remember the wrongdoings of my parents (or parent figures) towards me, my self-talks are like these:

◦ Could it be that my parents (or parent figures) violated my physical, emotional, and/or sexual boundaries because they were *deeply troubled people* and needed help to deal with their *troubled childhood*?

◦ Could it be that my parents (or parent figures) underfunctioned for me because they had *limited external resources* (i.e., they lacked sufficient wealth, knowledge, or education)? If so, then could it be that my parents *did their best given their circumstances*?

◦ Is it possible that my parents (or parent figures) were uninvolved, neglectful, or emotionally detached because they had *remained emotionally stuck* and therefore, they had *limited internal resources* (i.e., they lacked empathy)?

◦ Is it possible that when I called them out on their hurtful behaviors, my parents (or parent figures) punished, controlled, and silenced me (e.g., they withdrew their love or they snapped, yelled, and shouted at me) because they lacked emotional resilience (i.e., they were *vulnerable to the feelings of shame*)? If so, then could it be that my parents *suffered from fragile self-esteem*?

◦ Is it possible that my parents (or parent figures) were controlling, critical, and demeaning because they wanted me to behave in ways that would reflect well on them (as though I didn't matter or others were more important than me)? If so, then could it be that my parents *suffered from low self-esteem* (i.e., they needed to be affirmed by others that they were good enough) and *lacked healthy personal boundaries* (i.e., they imposed their own unhealthy standards onto me since they saw me as an extension of themselves)?

◦ Is it possible that, when I didn't meet their demands, my parents (or parent figures) punished, reproached, and guilted me (as though I was not a good person) since they *struggled with a sense of entitlement* (i.e., they believed that they deserved special treatment or recognition)? If so, then could it be that my parents *suffered from an exaggerated sense of self-importance* (i.e., they needed others to obey and be attentive to their demands in order to gain a sense of inner normalcy)?

◦ Could it be that that my parents (or parent figures) constantly faulted me (as though I was not good enough) because they *struggled with anxiety* that stemmed from *perfectionism*? If so, then could it be that my parents *suffered from an unhealthy sense of self-identity* (i.e., they needed to be perfect in order to feel worthy) and *lacked healthy personal boundaries* (i.e., they imposed their unrealistic standards of perfectionism onto me since they saw me as an extension of themselves)?

◦ Is it possible that my parents (or parent figures) kept

over functioning for me (as though I was incapable or inadequate) because they suffered from *low self-worth* (i.e., they needed to matter and be needed in order to feel worthy and gain a sense of inner normalcy)?

- Is it possible that one of my parents (or parent figures) didn't relate to me or that they treated me differently than my other siblings because they *saw me as an extension of my other parent, whom they resented?* If so, then could it be that this parent struggled with *emotional maturity* (i.e., they were unable to deal with their own negative emotions in a healthy manner)?

> Please take a few deep breaths and bring yourself to the present moment.
>
> While reading the following script, let each sentence deep into your conscious awareness.

These insights help me
realize that:

*Perhaps, my parents had remained unaware;
Therefore, they didn't know any better.*

This understanding mindset empowers me
to become more forgiving.

Now,

I reject my parents' flawed character-traits,
not them.

Now,

*I forgive my parents for their past
wrongdoings towards me.*

*I forgive my parents for their dysfunctional parenting
style that shaped my character flaws.*

*I forgive my parents for all the things that I have
blamed and resented them for.*

*Forgiving my parents allows me to release
my deep emotional pain.*

*Forgiving my parents heals me
and helps me move onward.*

Now,

*I no longer blame my parents for my present
emotional sufferings.*

Now,

*I'm empowered to retake my personal power
and see that I have choices.*

---

*Please pause, take a few deep breaths
and bring yourself to the present moment.*

*While continuing to read the following
script, let each sentence deep into
your conscious awareness.*

*Then, allow the Nurturing Adult
within you to guide you.*

Although I now understand my parents' experiences,
accept their humanness, and
forgive them for their wrongdoings,
I do *not* condone their hurtful behaviors;

Nor do I live a passive life and
allow myself to get hurt over and over again.

Now,
I realize that:

As an adult, I am not weak, helpless,
or defenseless.

Therefore, I no longer see myself as a *helpless child*
who needs to be pitied, protected, or defended.

Now,
I realize that:

As an adult, I am responsible for my own
emotional experiences and happiness.

Therefore, I no longer tell grievance stories in which
I blame my parents for all my problems.

Now,
I realize that:

As an adult, I am not trapped;
I have choices:

I *can* live a proactive and fulfilled life.

Therefore, I no longer feel stuck and seek comfort
in food, alcohol, or other substances . . .

Now,

While I forgive my parents for their past wrongdoings,
I stay in touch with my own *self* and identify with my
own thoughts, experiences, and feelings.

This self-empathy empowers me to stay
secure and strong.

Now,

Instead of blaming, I hold my parents accountable
in an assertive way:

I share my feelings, thoughts, and realities
directly, straightforwardly, and firmly,
in a respectful, non-reactive, and
non-provocative manner.

Now,

I protect myself by defining and establishing
a set of healthy personal boundaries.

Now,

I follow through and maintain the constructive
limits that I set *consistently*.

*Please pause
for reflection.*

While we forgive others for their wrongdoings towards us, we stay in touch with our own *self* and identify with our own thoughts, experiences, and feelings. This self-empathy empowers us to stay secure and strong and lead a proactive life.

Forgiveness is about letting go of resentment and the urge to fix or punish those who have mistreated you. Forgiveness is *not* about going back when there is no accountability. Forgiveness is *not* about sticking around and getting hurt time and time again.

Forgiveness is about accepting others' humanness. Forgiveness is *not* about excusing, rationalizing, or justifying hurtful behaviors.

Forgiveness frees you:
When you forgive, you will see your choices.

"Forgiveness doesn't excuse their behaviors. Forgiveness prevents their behavior from destroying your heart."—Unknown

> *Please pause a moment. Take a slow and deep breath. While reading the following script, let each sentence deep into your conscious awareness. Then, allow the Nurturing Adult within you to guide you.*

Now,
I believe in myself and recognize the strength and the wisdom within me.

Now,
I overcome my feelings of resentment that have stopped me from living a fulfilled life.

Now,
I don't relive the past to fix it.

Now,
I let go of my *anger*.

Now,
I let go of all my *feelings of resentment*.

Now,
I let go of the feelings of *guilt* and *shame*.

Now,
I love myself unconditionally.

> "Forgiveness is giving up all hope of a better past."
> —Jack Kornfeld

> *Please stay in the present moment!*

> "Holding on to anger is like grasping a hot coal with the intent of throwing it at someone else; You are the one who gets burned."
> —Buddha

> Forgiveness offers us a sense of serenity and inner calmness.

> Forgiveness happens through time: It follows naturally when we gain insight and develop an understanding and accepting mindset towards ourselves and other people.

> While such measures as meditation, counseling, or anger-management training could bring about a sense of calmness, in the absence of *true forgiveness*, they may not result in a *lasting emotional healing*.

> We know that we have reached a state of true forgiveness and emotional healing when our emotional anguish is replaced with a sense of emotional liberation; our anger with inner peace; and, our deep resentment with goodwill.

> *Please pause a moment. Take a slow and deep breath. While reading the following script, let each sentence deep into your conscious awareness. Then, allow the Nurturing Adult within you to guide you.*

Now that I understand the past better;
Now that I've gained more insight into
myself and others;
Now that I've forgiven myself for
my past wrongdoings;
Now that I've learned from my past mistakes;
Now that I've forgiven those who have
wronged me; and,
Now that I've put the painful past behind me,
I can live in the here and now.

To discover your *True Self*, make peace with the past.

Look into the past to learn from what it teaches you about the present. Then, leave it where it belongs: Past belongs to the past.

When we ruminate and dwell on the past, we end up suffering from depression.

Look into the future to help you make better choices in the present. Then, leave it where it belongs: Future belongs to the future.

When we worry and think excessively about the future, we may end up suffering from anxiety.

Take a slow and deep breath and stay in the present moment!

Summary

Now that I am more enlightened,
I acknowledge and accept my humanness and
forgive myself for my past wrongdoings.

Now, I no longer judge, label, or depreciate
myself when I make a mistake;
Instead, I hold myself accountable and
commit to new ways of being.

As I extend this conscientious and empathetic
state of mind towards others, I acknowledge
and accept other people's humanness and
forgive those who have wronged me.

Now, when I'm wronged, I don't hold grudges,
feel self-pity, or form grievance stories;
Instead, I hold others accountable in a non-reactive,
non-provocative, and constructive way.

Now that I am more enlightened,
I understand that our imperfections and
character flaws don't define or devalue any of us;

However, I realize that when we remain unaware
and live on autopilot, we may be judged, labeled,
rejected, or abandoned for our mindless ways of being.

Accepting the truth that no one is perfect frees me
from having high expectations;
Now, I realize that holding myself or others to
unrealistic standards leads to the feelings of
disappointment, resentment, and emotional pain.

PERCEPTIVE SELF-TALKS

Now that I am more enlightened,
I realize that I'm not trapped:
I *have* choices; I *can* heal my emotional pain.

Now,

I feel liberated and empowered
to engage in self-care.

Now,

I will keep moving forward to fulfill my vision.

> Kindness and empathy are *not* signs of weakness or naivety.
> The ability to understand others and express positive emotions is reflective of a growth mindset and strong sense of '*Self*.'
> *To practice empathy: Observe, Think, Feel!*

> "Who you are becoming is more important than who you have been."—Robyn Sharma

> *Stay in the present moment and allow the Nurturing Parent within you to guide you.*

> Retake your personal power:
> Your emotional experiences don't have
> to result in emotional suffering.

Accountability and Empowerment: A Four-Step Strategy for Overcoming Resentment

Accountability and Empowerment helps you gain insight into yourself:

> *Are you feeling offended? Are you feeling annoyed?*
>
> *Are you comparing yourself and feeling that you're less than others?*
>
> *Do you feel that you've been wronged?"*

Through inspiring you to look inwardly, this *transformational* book empowers you to retake your personal power, see all your choices, let go of the feelings of anger and resentment, and live a proactive life.

> *Accountability and Empowerment: A Four-Step Strategy for Overcoming Resentment* is a must-read book for those who are experiencing resentment at home, at work, towards parents, friends, or others; searching for answers; craving for inner peace; or, struggling to maintain weight loss or sobriety.

Books Published by A. Sehatti

BUILDING A STRONG SENSE OF SELF
Embarking on the Journey of Change
The Inner Control Is the True Control - Book 1

ACCOUNTABILITY AND EMPOWERMENT
A Four-Step Strategy for Overcoming Resentment
The Inner Control Is the True Control - Book 2

A TOOL FOR LETTING GO OF RESENTMENT AND ANGER
Short. Straightforward. Transformative.

A WORKBOOK FOR OVERCOMING RESENTMENT
Mindfulness Scripts

A HANDBOOK FOR DEALING WITH SUGAR CRAVINGS AND DEPENDENCY
NCWC's Nutrition 101 Series

NCWC'S NUTRITION 101 WORKBOOK
NCWC's Nutrition 101 Series

21-DAY LOG BOOK FOR ACHIEVING WELLNESS GOALS
NCWC's Nutrition 101 Series

www.ingramcontent.com/pod-product-compliance
Lightning Source LLC
Chambersburg PA
CBHW071831290426
44109CB00017B/1797